I0471445

The 51st State of Mind

MY VISION TO FIX CHICAGO AND BEYOND

John Q Public

ISBN-13: 9781492920960
ISBN-10: 1492920967

THE TRUTH, THE WHOLE TRUTH AND NOTHING BUT THE TRUTH.

This project started out with one clear intention. The next chapter of my life would be devoted to saving by beloved city from destruction and implosion.

The idea seemed simple enough. I would place my basic plans and guidelines in a simple format. I would expose this to the general public. After some public discourse and presuming my plan is in fact viable, I can elevate it to the next level and actually get something done.

Was it a pipe dream? I never thought so. Crazier things can happen. So phase one started. I wrote my little book, It is short, sweet and definitely radical. But we live in very challenging times. One must think outside the box.

My plan was to take my completed manuscript and show it to three specific acquaintances within my inner circle. Each one carries a unique skillset that I was convinced would green light my master plan.

I presented the manuscript to person one, as I handed it over we both sat down. I simply said please read this. It took the person about thirty minutes to read. When done I simply asked "what do you think"

The first comment was, "It isn't a book it is a skeleton", next comment was "It won't sell outside "Chicago", I asked if there were any other comments and the reply was "I didn't understand two chapters"

I was unhappy, I realize it is an unconventional approach to deliver a message but what was more upsetting is that no specific topics, claims or ideas were mentioned. I did not prod for certain information, I was so convinced that the information spoke for itself that I purposely planned on saying nothing.

This was strike one. Person number two was a multi-purpose reviewer. Firstly this person is a Newsie personified and a certifiable political junkie. Secondly after a glowing review my plan was to have this person clean up my book and fix my one main weakness, "punctuation"

The person flew through the book in 20 minutes. The body language and the constant rolling of the eyes were devastating. When finished this person tore into me like I was insane. Accused me of being a racist. Said I trampled on the Bill of Rights and was amazed someone was capable of penning such crap and lies.

And that great experience brings us to number three. Although number three is the one person I know the least. This person was to be the pinnacle of my research. I know this person through a good friend. This person has already published one book and started a billion dollar company. This person is very well respected and agreed through our mutual acquaintance to review my work. Since the manuscript was raw and unedited I opted to email it for review.

Twenty four hours later I received my response. It was an eloquent letter stating the challenges a writer faces in order to publish. Also included were many helpful tips on writing comparing the process to a grand meal that starts with a basic recipe. It goes on to mention that this person's sixteen chapter book was a twelve year labor of love.

That was my grand experiment. Three diverse intelligent people and nobody said nothing about the actual meat, only the potatoes. I sat on this project for several weeks pondering different solutions. I wanted to publish it but I did not want to humiliate myself if in fact they are right and I am possibly crazy.

Then I came up with a compromise. I will release the book, raw, unedited and uncut. I will release it anonymously and let the public decide. If it flops I will go back to the drawing board. If it sails then I will come forward and working with all of you, we can start the revolution.

A couple of quick things. The official first chapter is where I hide my identity. If this book works that chapter will be released unedited.

Next, This entire project is not and never will be about money.

Although this is about Chicago, this applies to the entire country.

Lastly, This is not a flat out attempt to run for the office of Mayor of Chicago. I will gladly work with the existing administration to see these bold, radical plans to fruition. If the plans and programs are accepted and verified and local officials choose not embrace them, Then I will proudly take the next step.

Thanks for giving me a chance.

Sincerely,

John Q. Public
Johnqpublic2015@gmail.com

Always remember others may hate you but those who hate you don't win unless you hate them. And then you destroy yourself.

Richard M. Nixon, *in his White House farewell*
37th president of US (1913 - 1994)

INTRODUCTION

My adventure begins in the middle of April in 196█. I was welcomed into this world at ███████████████ Hospital in Chicago. I don't remember much of the events that day but it taught me one important lifelong lesson. I hate moving day!!

After a short stint in ████ ████████ ███, we were off to the suburbs. We settled in ███████████, Illinois.

For those of you trying to pre judge me I would like to point out that I am referring to the █████ of ███████████. And there I was, a basic middle class 1960's suburban family unit consisting of ████████ ████████████████. 1960'S Life was typically normal as I could understand. As I would later learn of the Vietnam War and the Kennedy and King assassinations it was a history lesson, not a real life experience.

In the winter of 1967, things must have been going good at home. We moved to the ████████ of ████████████ also known as the ███████████████. Let the judging begin. Moving into a better neighborhood in a bigger house did not immediately affect my persona or judgement. A 7 year old really doesn't absorb the big picture.

Turns out there was a big picture. I was Jewish, the neighborhood was not. Not only that but the neighborhood was primarily old school, old money Catholic and they apparently did not like Jews.

Not really understanding the issues at hand, I simply listened to my parents and stayed in the yard, we kept to ourselves. One winter my parents bought us all ice skates. The park down the block from us had a really nice ice rink and I wanted to go skating. One night a bunch of kids told me that Jews are not allowed at this park. Although I can't remember exactly how I felt or what I did, I do remember being tied to a tree at the park with someone's jump rope and beaten up.

Now let me clarify something. I am not one of these saps you would see on the Dr.Phil show crying about his horrible youth, that isn't me. Did these events shape my life? I am sure they did. As I matured and would read and study various forms of dysfunction I began to understand that every instance of every event positive or negative affects people. It is how people absorb and classify the data that makes people unique and perhaps subsequently successful versus failures, happy or sad.

As time progressed, the Jewish population increased. Virtually every Catholic retiring or moving out of the neighborhood would be replaced with a wealthy Jewish family. The balance of power never really changed because in those days, mainstream America appeared to fear what they did not know. Black America was not even part of our equation in the day.

I never grew up with strong religious beliefs. It was not mandated on me, we celebrated Christmas every year never Chanukah.

Not a religious Christmas mind you, simply Christmas morning we opened our gifts. Had a home cooked real hot breakfast, "including bacon" and played with our toys and gifts all day. The next day it was back to Captain Crunch.

There was one religious issue I could not escape however. I had to go to Hebrew school and have a

Bar Mitzvah. I am convinced this happened because my parents were simply keeping up appearances.

I trudged through five years of Hebrew school. Had a lavish Bar Mitzvah and never saw a dime of the loot. Go figure.

The only other time the Jewish factor entered my radar was during the time the ████████ tried to ████████ ████████. I remember passing the ████████████ Inn one morning on the way to school and watching the Jewish Defense League unloading their vans in the parking lot. I recall it pointed out to me that the JDL's weapon of choice was the baseball bat.

The summer after I graduated my junior year of ████████ high school in ████████████ed devastating news. We would be moving this summer.

I always existed in my faux cocoon of life, I never actually feared change because I was never exposed to it. This move would change all that. Having always felt sorry for new school transplants growing up I would now become one. What made matters more troubling is that this would be my last year of high school. I had never planned on attending college so this was it. The thought of moving out of state was very mentally trying on me.

Within days I was enlisted to push the for sale sign into our front lawn. As I pushed the sign in the grass I felt the pressure being lifted. For some strange reason I now welcomed this move. Within weeks our caravan of cars and a moving truck were heading ███ miles north to the little town of ███████, ██████████.

The only real memory I have of that day was when we finally turned on the television, the news had just broken that Elvis Presley had died. No real significance in my life but that ended day one.

I surprisingly adapted well to life in rural America. The people of ██████████ were great, I made friends quickly and actually enjoyed the lifestyle. School was fine, it was very different then city life but I got it, I related to it. As much I was enjoying life I was on the countdown to leave. I had one year of school left and I had planned to return to the Chicago area. I did not really have a plan or idea what I was going to do but I knew I was leaving. My basic idea was that I was going to become a ██████. My father had bought and older ████████████ years ago and I loved ██████ ██ with it. There was also a large █████████████ across from my junior high school and I loved hanging around after school. I think what really put me over the top was a great story my uncle told me years ago.

██

████████████████████████████

Around the intersection of Devon & Kedzie they get into an accident. ████████████████████████████████

██

██

██

████████████████████████████████

Come the following June it was all over. I graduated high school, I had physical possession of my diploma. That following night the graduating class threw a party at a club in ████████ ████████

We danced and drank and had a great time. When the party ended for whatever reason I drove home. I packed most of my worldly belongings in my yellow Toyota Corolla and I drove to Chicago.

I arrived around 600am, I had found a flea bag motel in ████████████ and I set up camp. I quickly began to realize that I was not prepared to be there and as I would meet with old acquaintances and try to formulate a plan, time and money were quickly running out.

At that point I was struck with an Epiphany. Possibly the first but certainly not the last I would experience throughout my life. I packed up the car and I headed back to ████████.

The epiphany was a book I owned. The book was the "The Success System that Never Fails" written by W. Clement Stone. Now I would be lying if I told you when, where and why I bought this book. I simply do not remember now and I do not recall remembering then. I was aware it was in my possession and for whatever reason I was guided. I was on my way back ████████ to retrieve it.

I arrived in ████████ , found the book, took a long nap and returned to Chicago. Settling back at the ████████████ Motel I read the book. I can't recall whether there were fireworks or what it is a hazy memory. What I do remember was the following morning I put on my graduation suit. I then drove my 18 year old self over to ████████████████████████ . I knocked on the door and met the owner ████████████ .

████████ appeared to have a preconception of a young kid over-reaching his desires but we chatted. He appeared either amused or amazed at the history of the industry I have already mastered. I then began to amaze or amuse him with my knowledge of the ████████████████ . The Chicago area at the time was really on the forefront of the development of the ████████████████ ████████ industry.

Like I told him, I was never into ████████ , This was my thing. After about 90 minutes of chatting, he excuses himself and goes inside his office. He emerges a few minutes later with an Illinois Bell Pageboy.

For those of you youngsters out there, this was one of the first single tone "beepers" used in the 70's.

He hands it to me and says, Ok ████████ you are hired.

Needless to say I was ecstatic, I had a job, a job in the industry I chose. Now I could go on and on and detail the ups and the downs and my hundreds of ▮▮▮ with ▮▮ but I hate to bore you.

I will however mention two ironic things. Firstly within about a year of starting

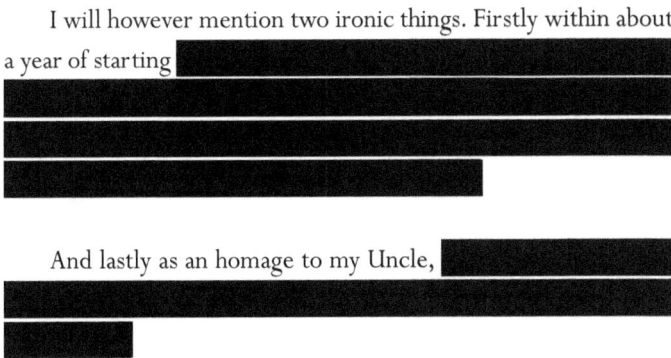

And lastly as an homage to my Uncle, ▮▮▮▮▮▮▮

And that brings us to today. I have spent 30 years in the business. Started as a ▮▮▮▮ and I have performed at all levels of labor and management. Written articles, started and participated in State and National Associations and trade groups. ▮▮▮▮▮▮▮ ▮▮▮. Worked with the ▮▮▮▮▮ industry on the design, manufacture and marketing of ▮▮▮ and I am also involved in the history of the industry working with the media worldwide on stories and the retrospective on the industry as a whole.

It was a good run, I made great friends, made some enemies along the way. I helped and mentored many, I was helped and mentored as well. I made many bad decisions, did things I regret. But all in all I stimulated the economy, made a living and generally had a blast along the way.

I have always planned on starting a new career on my 50th birthday. When I turned 50 I started procrastinating. The recession was starting to lift and as usual the industry was going through another midlife crisis so I kept going. Within a year or so I had finally made my decision. I then started to plan my exit strategy to jump start my new career.

And that brings us to today.

After much soul searching and thought, I have decided to devote the next chapter in my life to public service. There are numerous ways that people give back to society. Some loudly donate to charity, many quietly donate to charity. Some give blood, some work at food banks. Many give and support various forms of public service through their houses of worship.

I suppose it is all a matter of semantics, while the police and firefighters are public servants I think members of the armed forces would be considered public service. I think all people have a certain part of their brain which makes them want to help their fellow man. It is a real feel good. Many people make lifetime careers of giving. Most corporations have charitable donations in their budgets.

The form of public service I have chosen is to enter politics. The process to enter politics is basic and fill in the blank easy. However in Chicago and more specifically the State of Illinois it takes on a whole different dynamic. Politics around here is a contact sport, it is more who you know, not what you know or what your plans and ideas are. If you plan on even trying to modify the status quo you are inviting trouble. The reason those concepts will not faze me is because I have a new concept. I have formulated a business model to govern, and fix the problems that virtually every county, village, town and municipality suffers from. This concept is so revolutionary that the master plan entails rebuilding the entire Country from the inside out utilizing Chicago at the core.

Before I get into specific details, I want to make a few things clear. The super majority of this country is in severe financial crisis. Every election cycle a new group of candidates promises to go to

City Hall, the State house, the Congress, Senate or whatever and reform, reform and reform. I really truly in my heart believe they want to create change, I really trust and in many cases can see and feel their passion. However I am convinced that the current state of government renders them moot. The system doesn't tolerate or allow real people to make real change.

Like most Americans, politically I was a casual observer a good portion of my life. I started studying and following politics more intently in my early thirties. I identified myself jointly as Reagan Republican and a Daley Democrat. Life was good and the country and our economy buzzed along fine. As 24 hour cable news made their mark on the American lexicon I almost became addicted to the news. With the advent of the internet and more importantly Wikipedia I became a voracious reader in current events.

Politically things did not always go to my thought, positions or desires. Like many Americans you swear, you get pissed and basically engage in the lively art of discussion and move on. Sometimes you revert to the "nothing I can do about anyways" theory. Very rarely in our history of politics, at least the last 25 years can many politicians really be remembered for groundbreaking acts or major policy reforms.

The old adage is the first day in office most politicians work on their re-election.

I started getting restless around the time that Fox news started gaining stride as a news leader. At first I thought this was Wally George in the new millennium. Then I began to see that people, many people, smart people were really taking them seriously. I just did not get it. I remember when Journalism was a noble profession.

I was not quite understanding how this Country was adapting and more importantly adopting this style of news propaganda.

I tried not to let this bother me. Although I didn't believe I was a liberal person I had to watch MSNBC so I could be educated and kept informed. The anchors on MSNBC were talented and intelligent. But while FOX was growing, better yet bulldozing them, MSNBC would causally report of FOX's claims and controversies and then people like Bill Maher and John Stewart would actually make a living entertaining smart people by showing them what stupid people watch.

I needed a rest, Life was good. Barack Obama was elected President and Rahm Emanuel was elected our mayor. I felt good, I felt covered. I am a huge fan of both. I had full faith and confidence in the pair to look after people like me locally and Nationally.

We needed new leadership at the start of President Obama's term. Our country was ravaged by a war and the housing crisis decimated our economy. I remember when George W. Bush was re-elected the Daily Mail in London had a headline claiming American's were crazy. Were we bullied into re-electing him?, Were we scared into the re-electing him?. More importantly did Fox News run cover for the entire eight year debacle.

President Obama had a great honeymoon, the press was respectful as we got to know him. The Republicans licked their wounds in private. The entire world seemed to like him and respect our country. Certainly being black was part of it. But from my standpoint this man stood up and did the impossible. He pulled off what nobody thought was ever going to happen.

Then it got ugly. I compare the ugly to our invasion of Iraq. I remember the day our tank knocked down the Saddam Hussein statue. I watched as all of the Iraqi's were jubilant in the street, chasing down the statue as it was dragged and hitting it with their shoes. "I sign of disrespect". Turns out I was all wrong. What I was not wrong about was that the Iraq people truly were ecstatic, for a fleeting moment they actually thought good was upon them. Unbeknownst to them, the evildoers had scattered and were in hiding. They would eventually return and rear their ugly heads and almost destroy our initial mission and permanently scar our reputation.

The same thing happened as President Obama's honeymoon ended. Our evildoers also went into hiding. When they reared their ugly heads several weeks later they pulled off what I consider to be the greatest marketing fete since the pet rock. They convinced mainstream America that our economy is in ruins, your house will be foreclosed and your jobs are gone because you elected a Nigger to the White House.

Guess what, They bought it. Hook line and sinker. With Fox news running cover the talking heads arrived en masse and convinced millions that they screwed up. What about Bush + 8.

When Glen Beck goes on television and claims he thinks President Obama hates white people I knew we were in big trouble.

If those issues were not disheartening enough to me, I had even bigger issues. I voted for Rahm Emanuel because he had a great reputation. He was known as the go to guy. A behind the scenes genius. He was like Lee Atwater without the horns, Like Karl Rove with class. A true overachiever and American success story. He has Washington credentials, big business cred. I was a very early supporter. I had heard stories about him such as mailing the dead fish. All good by me. A tough politician is my politician.

When the King Maker decides to become King. They can bank on my vote.

As the Mayoral election process started Rahm got off to a rocky start. The established Lasalle Street crew would have none of this. While other candidates tried to get invited to the party it was obvious this was Rahm's election. Then the residency issue became the cause celebre. By the time Rob Halpin entered the race to further confuse things it became obvious that this had Ed Burke DNA all over it.

When the courts finally cleared his path to become Mayor I said on many occasions that Ed Burke will regret the day he messed with Rahm. Nobody messes with the Rahminator.

I figured the first thing Mayor Emmanuel would do after taking office was removing Alderman Burke's security detail for proper punishment. I was wrong. The way I now look at it, those Police officers essentially got a raise by virtue of keeping their jobs. Next Rahm Emmanuel takes on Karen Lewis.

Karen Lewis responds by pimp slapping him with a stupid stick. I am sorry but I am suffering from a horrible case of buyer's remorse. I really thought I was being looked after. What started as a great decade was becoming my worst nightmare.

These are many of the reasons I want to enter politics. I however, have new, ambitious, ground breaking, game changing plans to make a better world. But where do I begin? Illinois Governor ? Cook County Board ? Mayor of Chicago?

The state, County and city are three broke entities living off each other in quasi dysfunctional triage similar to Siamese triplets sharing one brain with three greed genes. They may be unable to survive independently but definitely are unable to play nice as a group. What I keep trying to convince myself is the goal is pleasing the voters. That is a tough nut to crack these days with the jaded state of our voters.

So I have decided to take a new novel approach. I will put my plans and ideas out there.

I will leave it up to you.

Before I explain my plans and timeline I must make numerous points straight and very clear so you understand where I am coming from and what I want to do. I will further explain in more detail in the following chapters.

Chicago is a city in serious trouble. The survival and future of Chicago are related directly to fiscal health and welfare of Cook County Government and the State of Illinois Government as a whole.

Cook County and the State of Illinois are in as serious trouble as Chicago. Without reform and change across the board it will be difficult for one to succeed without the others. As my platform will show, part of the plan is to spread my business model across the country as the program matures.

Basically I plan on reinventing a modern metropolis and country from the inside out.

We have a pension crisis. I will tell you now, There is no plausible plan possible to fix it overnight. This problem was many years in the making and it would take many more years to fix it if it can be fixed at all.

Chicago like most of America has an antiquated infrastructure. Repairing old technology is like throwing good money after bad. We need new modern infrastructure to last the next 100 years. An infrastructure that is scalable and offers multiple uses within the City's framework and is poised for National growth and integration.

Our school system, police and fire try to compete operationally, functionally and financially using old school parameters in a modern society. A complete revamp is needed.

Jump starting Chicago's position as the future First City with six massive public works programs.

Multi-Modal transit & transportation network.

Rebuilt Police and Fire departments.

A new School System.

The Chicago Medical Partnership.

Tri-State overseas Highway.

Intercoastal Waterway.

MULTI-MODAL TRANSIT & TRANSPORTATION NETWORK

The city of Chicago, similar to any major city hosts a web of light rail and heavy rail commuter transit options. We also maintain suburban heavy commuter rail, commercial cargo railroads, Amtrak and O'hare's people mover system.

These various forms of transportation all share many common denominators. They are all based on slightly modernized versions of very old technology. With the exception of some track sharing, all the systems have no interchangeability. And with the probable exception of the freight trains, they all lose money.

We need a new system that incorporates all present and future light and heavy rail needs incorporated into a new state of the art rail network.

I propose the Multi-Modal transit & transportation network, hereinafter referred to as xMODALx.

The primary first purpose is to fund, design and build the system within the city of Chicago. The secondary plan is to have cities all over the country adapt the same network. Within several years actual cities will be able to link each system together as we slowly encompass North America.

The xMODALx can and will revolutionize mass transit.

The first step is to work in conjunction with the Federal Transit Administration in order to establish guidelines on track type and size. The United States has hundreds of rail systems all over the country utilizing between 4 to 10 different track gauges. In order to bring North America up to date we need the Federal Transit Administration to establish time limits and guidelines to develop multi gauge track that will eventually support a new mandated limited amount of rail chassis sizes.

The subterranean or elevated tubes that comprise the network will also contain new sewer pipes that will eventually replace our antiquated sewer system. There will be fresh water pipes to store, move, and displace water where and when needed. "In the future, water will surpass oil as a guarded natural resource" Finally a super bundle will include natural gas lines, electric lines, high speed cable and copper wire. This installation will facilitate the growth and replacement of our older infrastructure and it will be in place, protected from the environment the way it should be. A city without power lines and utility poles will free up an amazing amount of real estate and render Chicago weatherproof.

There are numerous other additions and features that can retrofitted into the xMODALx business model. There are already numerous personal rapid transit prototypes being developed and I even foresee a spare bedroom in a home can be put on a flatbed, taken to a xMODALx station and that replaces a motor home. It can even be sent to a family's vacation home in Florida and reattached

For the season. The possibilities are endless.

All new buildings, schools, stadiums and commercial construction would incorporate xMODALx terminals within their new construction. The future network would eliminate all large truck and bus traffic and severely decrease vehicular movement.

However, the piece de resistance of the xMODALx will be the collection and distribution of our cities waste. Between scattered consumer trash centers to actual xMODALx trash cars that enter commercial and government buildings. The network will collect and transport our cities waste to recycling centers and landfills. The current process of door to door trash pick-up by municipalities and private haulers is

A innefective process.

As the xMODALx begins to reach it mark, and as the old CTA as we know begins to disappear I plan on retrofitting old CTA lines with xMODALx carriages to build an underground safe zone evacuation center that will work in conjunction with the network. Chicago as it stands is nowhere near prepared for natural disaster or acts of war. The old CTA underground infrastructure could be converted to house at least a half a million people with numerous entry and exit points throughout the city.

PUBLIC SAFETY OFFICERS

Public safety officers, hereinafter referred to as PSO's would be the future model in a modern municipal

City. A PSO would be cross trained as a police officer, a firefighter and an EMT. These civil servants will be able to rotate their shifts around the three professions. It will allow more flexible scheduling among the three departments. This would be ideal during special events, weather emergencies, natural disasters and wars. When Chicago has a major fire the police are limited to traffic control and subsequent investigations. Granted they perform many lifesaving acts as well as the firefighters but having all three professions crossed trained is a natural fit. It will also dramatically cut down on the repetition workers often face in their long careers.

Training all existent department members for this scenario would not be feasible. It would apply to all new hires under a new training mandate. I would also like to implement a new cadet program that will efficiently breed and train new hires. Why the police department in particular has had problems attracting new officers has always mystified me.

The cadet program would begin similar to the ROTC where high school students could participate. The students could eventually wind up within the city but also have the option to go into the military. They would also be cadet staff members of their school security detail during their time in school.

A cadet that decides to enter the City of Chicago PSO program, would start a three year apprentice program working amongst the three departments. They would be paid a nominal wage and work hands on with veteran PSO's. I envision every police car having one trained officer and one cadet while on patrol. This will give Chicago a large instant police presence increase.

A well rounded new generation metropolitan police force cannot possibly be effective without a functional relationship with the populous. When the authorities were narrowing down the Boston Marathon bomber they ordered everybody to stay inside. With my vision if we had a similar situation, the 911 center would send out an Amber alert type mass message which would be a call to arms.

The responders would be a combination of block clubs, off duty PSO's, armed and non-armed citizens, similar to a Militia type organization or neighborhood watch group that is approved by and works under the auspices of the City. Working together they can provide law enforcement with thousands of more eyes and ears to keep the city safe.

In a perfect world, I would have liked to see all inclusive PSO stations, all new, all large, all xMODALx friendly, perhaps built within our new super schools, (see next chapter) but that may not be feasible at this time. There are numerous new police and fire stations recently built and this would require much more time and study.

One big issue that has financially decimated our city is the constant lawsuits filed against the Police department. The process is tantamount to winning the lottery. The only way we can move forward is with a simple understanding and a new law.

The understanding is simple. Police take an oath to serve and protect. They are human. They make mistakes. Friendly fire happens locally and certainly within the military. A police officer could be on his sixth year without a blemish on his record yet nobody goes out of their way to say thanks. Then one night while protecting us he is approached by a man in the alley. The officer's gun is drawn, there was a shooting in the neighborhood minutes earlier. The man reaches into his pocket and the officer is convinced it is a gun, as the man pulls it out the officer shoots and kills the man. Turns out it was a cell phone. The dead man has a rap sheet. His mother goes on TV to tell everybody how much of a gentleman he is. The lawyers race to mama and two years later she gets four million dollars of our money. Now enters the Police review board and internal affairs. Now the police officer is guilty until proven innocent and he swears never to shoot again. Let the truth be told. I want my officers to shoot. I do not want them to be afraid. People, mistakes can and will happen.

The city needs and require a simple arbitration clause. When you live here, when you work here, when you visit here, You cannot sue the Board of education, fire department or the police department unless the act caused upon you is deemed egregious.

Currently, the biggest problem the City of Chicago is facing is our street gangs.

All levels of government and the clergy have wrestled with ideas and solutions to solve this problem.

One must realize and understand, gang members are enemies of the state.

Not too long along Senator Mark Kirk and Representative Bobby Rush met and announced that with twenty million dollars they would fix the problem.

The way to solve the street gang issue is firstly put things in the proper perspective. Gang bangers are like rats. To get rid of rats you need a simple three prong approach. Firstly you cut off their food source.

It is my uneducated guess, my personal non substantiated theory that the majority of all gang bangers are on public assistance in one form or the other. If any gang banger is arrested, suspected or claims gang affiliation they will lose any and all public assistance from the city, the county, the state and the federal government. If the gang banger has children at home and the family relies on assistance, they will also lose any and all benefits. If the gang banger lives with grandma who is a stellar retired citizen on a fixed income and he is arrested, Grandma will lose everything. Word will spread, keep your family in check. No family members will be able to walk away unscathed. They brought the gang bangers here. They are just as culpable. We must also utilize the RICO act in all levels of gang enforcement and termination.

Included but not limited to taking possession of all personal belongings, possessions and property of offenders, we will also include landlords and property managers that knowingly rent to gang affiliated tenants and their agents.

Secondly, Chicago will pass a home rule law where we can evict residents form our city. Any gang banger arrested, convicted or who admits gang affiliation will be evicted from the city along with their immediate family or dependents. As a going away gift They will all receive a one way bus ticket to anywhere outside of Illinois.

The third process involves limiting procreation.

Gang bangers have time to gang bang because they choose not to go to work.

They choose welfare over work.

In the end. With perfect execution and community involvement. I foresee ridding the city of it's street gangs and reducing the crime rate in epic proportions. If you look at the statistics from the Chicago crime commission's recent book and do a little math. I was just thinking we can save the taxpayers, say around twenty million the first couple years.

Lastly, I would like to see the new department exist without a labor union. I am not pro union, I am certainly not anti-union. Unions add costs, we need to do more with less. A city hall that respects it's civil servants and desires for them to succeed can certainly come to terms in a proper and professional manner. I am not looking to split the difference. I want all of our employees to be the highest paid in their fields nationally. It is good for morale, it is good for future residents who want to move here, it will help cement our reputation as America's new first city. However I would love to do a study on rerouting the savings to help save the pension plans.

CHICAGO PUBLIC SCHOOLS

The Chicago Public School system suffers from a myriad of problems as do many other large school systems. The basic elements of running a large school district have not changed much over the years.

Typical issues like class size, teacher pay, cutting programs and other items plaque our school systems.

There never is and never will be enough funding in a major city for teachers to give their best and students to get the best a modern educator is trained to deliver. Many parents around the country opt for private schools to ensure their children get a quality and safe education.

I truly believe I can create an inner city educational center of excellence by utilizing a complete new radical approach to educating our children. This will be done in a multi-phase 15 year plan.

There are currently 600 elementary and high schools in the Chicago board of education.

My plan is to reduce it to 10 schools. We will begin with PS-1, PS-2, PS-3 and PS-4 which obviously

Stands for public school 1 and so forth. For better edification we will refer to these facilities as PSX.

The first PSX will be built in Warren Park on the far North side. Although the 90 acre area is a little less than I am comfortable with, there are many apartment and commercial buildings on it's south and east border which may be purchased at a later time to increase the footprint.

The second PSX would be in Humboldt Park, the third in Marquette Park and the final in Calumet Park.

To be clear, These properties will cease being parks and become school campuses. The Chicago Park district has 570 parks throughout the City. We will remove approximately thirty five percent of their real estate holdings.

Once phase two begins, the remaining 6 campuses would be constructed on property formerly used as parks, forest preserves and City Colleges. City Colleges will be integrated within the PSX campus's after the first year in operation. There is ample real estate to go around and ample real estate to liquidate upon a complete revamp and rebuild.

Each PSX campus will contain the following.

A complete PSO station housing Police, fire and EMT's. As I mentioned before with the recent new Police and fire stations recently built this will be up for further analysis.

The department of Children and Family Services currently maintain 17 offices within the City. I would like to help them save money and help our students with their service and support by having a DCFS office within each campus. It also gives them a better proximity to the PSO station.

We will have a complete state of the art gym facility and stadium(s) within each campus. Sports and fitness for kindergarten through college must be the best available.

A multi denominational house of worship

A state of the art library that will be open to the public.

A Chicago medical partnership office

Hostel for troubled or displaced kids, weather emergencies and out of district and state tuition students.

Each classroom will have one accredited teacher with a 100:1 ratio.

One teacher aide working as apprentices within a City College of Chicago program will be in each room

We will have 2 illiterate adults in each room working as aides to the teacher and assistant. One adult will be a Chicago resident, The other aide will be an immigrant or foreign national. These two positions will be on a volunteer no pay basis. I have always wanted to find a place to help people suffering from illiteracy. These are good people with fully developed mature minds. By learning to read and write at the elementary level they can learn quickly while providing excellent teacher support and motivating the children to the importance of education. The foreign national or immigrant reason is while accomplishing the same goal they can also assist students trying to master the English language.

With the exception of the normal curriculum schools are required to teach. I want our PSX's to offer a more comprehensive approach to educating our youth. I want to inspire them and make them want to come to school and stay in school. One way I want to accomplish this is teaching under the guise of mob mentality where they learn and succeed as a group. Where the students will reach out to each other in need because it will become fashionable to succeed individually and as a class. By the same token they will be encouraged to respond in a crowdsource manner because they will understand their wants and needs are always welcome and respected.

Amongst the other additions to the curriculum are.

Social media,

Religious studies, tolerance and understanding.

How and when to report friends or families to the authorities

Basic health and birth control.

Life planning.

How to shop, how to cook, how to eat, c stores vs wharehouse clubs.

History of social welfare, public housing and it's effect on society.

Media history, watching Leave it to Beaver and the Cosby show and how it affects and molds our society past and present.

The state of the art library center will be designed for students in Kindergarten through college. The reason I mentioned that they will be open to the public is because the Chicago public library currently maintains 79 branches, add another 600 libraries in the schools and another 13 for City Colleges. That is inefficacious expensive overkill. Harold Washington will remain as the flagship but all others must be closed. Every student and citizen will travel a little farther but the Library's will be one of a kind.

As everybody is aware, Public schools do not charge parents for their child's education. Recently however many schools have been adding various surcharges, donations and other ways to maintain their product in a time of dwindling funds. Many parents do not like to pay. Some feel that they pay enough in taxes, others are simply too stupid to appreciate what a school tries to accomplish. The mentality that their parents never paid why should we still runs rampant in a soft society.

I have always thought that one of the reasons parents let their children skip an occasional day or even drop out early is because they do not appreciate something that they do not pay for. It is also fashionable to put down the school system because in their mind it is nothing more than a corrupt wing of a corrupt system. The teachers make more than they ever will and hope doesn't flow well among those not in tune with parental privilege.

However, when the average parent watches as this stunning 15 story school rises up. As they hear word on the street that this is Harvard for our kids. Then they find out there will be no service charges. No donations. Their kids will be getting a real education by a new school built for them. A real education they never had access to. They will be pleased and impressed and full of hope.

That brings us to tuition. When consumers pay for something they get a perception of value in return. They don't pay for school now and the communitie's confidence in all major school systems is consistently low. PSX tuition will be ten dollars per week. A student will get a first rate quality education that will exceed private schools charging in excess of one hundred dollars per week. Where some students used to use relatives addresses to get into suburban schools, this will now happen in reverse.

We will also open the school to non-city residents for a higher structured tuition. Parents will not so easily let the children miss classes or drop out because they now have financial interest in their education.

As far as my position on the teachers union. Please refer to the previous chapter.

As we close the smaller schools, colleges and librairies. I would like to see the properties become residential, commercial and light manufacturing. I would also like to emphasize the conversion of some schools to non-profit senior assisted living.

The current school budget is 5.5 billion dollars. The current City College budget is 503 million dollars.

The Chicago Library budget is 106 million dollars. The park district budget system wide is 385 million dollars. Now if you take 10 economists and tell them to crunch the numbers you will probably get 12 different answers. The bottom line is it will take a tremendous investment to start four PSX construction projects. The subsequent budget savings will be enormous. The cost per student even with tuition subsidization and followed by property liquidation and redevelopment will speak volumes for the project. I will leave the rest of this hypothesis to the experts.

THE CHICAGO MEDICAL PARTNERSHIP

Currently the City of Chicago provides health insurance to a minimum of sixty thousand employees which include teachers, police officers, firemen, Emt's and a variety of other city workers.

My proposal for Chicago Care begins with the basic framework of the city's current insurance program with is similar to any corporation who offers their employees a group plan. My plan entails adding many elements of the Romneycare plan which was enacted in 2006. Although Obamacare is a better more modern alternative it carries with it's name a stigma that certain groups refuse to endorse or approve since allowing President Obama to receive credit has been shown to give you cooties.

The purpose of adding and enhancing this to the architecture of Chicago's plan is to eventually provide insurance to all residents. Existing local companies would use Chicago Care to maintain employees and save money.

The key to developing a comprehensive medical network is to focus on the three main components that make it work.

Firstly, compelling people to enroll in a quality affordable program is not a challenge. The challenge is forming a program that works efficiently with specific guidelines.

Firstly, the program will be based on a pay for performance type model. A policy holder must adhere to a healthy lifestyle and get regular medical service and treatment. A substance abuser who frequents hospital E/R's for treatment. Then upon recovery returns to their bad habits will be surcharged out of the system or suspended.

A mildly overweight person will encouraged to lose weight or be surcharged accordingly. It is critical that members are to be serious about their health conditions. The basic health care problem is health conscious people pay for reckless people. It has been destroying the basic concept of managed health care for decades.

The administration of Chicago Care will be attained on many levels. As mentioned all PSX locations will have clinics, as hopefully would larger PSO stations and similar edifices. I would also love to entertain the idea of converting older empty hospitals to house larger clinics.

Lastly, The doctors, nurses and staff members need inducements to help start and launch a successful medical undertaking such as this. If Houses of worship are exempt from property taxes why can't our medical infrastructure and members enjoy the same privilege.

By working together to create a massive program with many in house features and functions. We can save money. Entice new business and residents and eventually sell the program to other towns and suburbs in the state.

XMODALX OVERSEAS HIGHWAY AND INTERCOASTAL WATERWAY

In order to jump start the National extension and promotion of the xMODALx system, I propose building a tri state overseas highway. The new highway Interstate 594 will begin in Milwaukee Wisconsin and travel South East towards Benton Harbor Michigan directly over Lake Michigan, in Benton harbor it will link up with the existing Interstate 94. This will open up a lucrative xMODALx rail, cargo and passenger route we have never been able to benefit from. It will significantly curtail inefficient commuter air routes as well.

This xMODALx highway we be a fully functioning, fully bundled track that will contain all purposes, options and benefits the xMODALx is capable of. At the half way point of the route, there will be a turn off that will send another four lane xMODALx line straight into the Chicago area. As the bypass approaches Chicago it will branch again giving the entire project a slightly warped (H) shape. The Southern North-South route will become Chicago's new intercoastal waterway, it will parallel Lake Shore Drive to the North.

It will allow exciting future development within the City. The existing Lake Shore Drive will be slightly modified to allow light commercial traffic and this will also negate the need to ever discuss the Crosstown expressway again. The residual effect will lighten all vehicular traffic as the developments proceed.

Once the engineers fine tune the plan, I would also like to incorporate the Eastern end of the link to work with the proposed Illiana Corridor and naturally convert that to xMODALx.

What I have not discussed in detail due to a complete lack of knowledge in the field is incorporating one or two world class suspension bridges within the framework of this concept.

PARETO PRINCIPLE

The **Pareto principle** (also known as the **80–20 rule**, the **law of the vital few,** and the **principle of factor sparsity**) states that, for many events, roughly 80% of the effects come from 20% of the causes

In regards to the Pareto Principle, My vision, my cause, my possible campaign will only be directed at eighty percent of Chicago's population.

It is my belief that 80% of Chicago works to support the 20% that don't.

I further believe that 80% of our troubles and crimes stem from the same 20%.

I cannot and will not invite them to my party. I wish to design the new capital of America for the 80% who deserve it. It is my further opinion that trying to fix the problem is nothing more than throwing good money after bad.

There comes a time when a City, a people must simply cut their losses and terminate the problem.

I do have sympathy, there are many situations where honest hard working people do indeed fall on hard times. That is why our Government set up numerous social safety nets. Unfortunately scores of people have used and abused the system for years and acted very badly in the process.

Before you hear them scream and protest, remember there is positively no excuse for third, fourth and fifth generation welfare clans. I am tired of the constant complaining of the perpetually poor and the wannabe working wounded. At the end of the day, I still pay their freight. No country, no city can move forward carrying this major expensive burden.

It brings to memory when I had a good friend visiting from out of town. We were driving through the Illinois Medical District. He marveled at the shiny new buildings and clean streets, It truly is an impressive area. He even mentioned to me it was like George Jetson's neighborhood.

As we traveled west outside of the district, he quipped. All right, back to the Flinstones.

The City of Chicago is truly a wonderful place. I am proud to call it my home.

Citizens of Chicago deserve so much better.

Hopefully, I may assist.

Sincerely,

Johnqpublic2015@gmail.com